la tetra o.

start GHETTO.

NO-NONSENSE GOAL SETTING FOR SELF-HELP HATERS

START GHETTO

She Dreams Co.

This book is not intended to be a substitute for professional advice, diagnosis, medical treatment, medication, or therapy. This text is not authorized to make recommendations about medication, spiritual guidance, or serve as a substitute for professional advice. Never disregard professional psychological or medical advice or delay in seeking professional advice or treatment because of something you've read in this or any self-help book.

Reformatted 1st Edition, September 2020

#startghetto

Dedication

For Charleston.

START GHETTO

Contents

START GHETTO

#startghetto FOREWORD

BY PHILIP ANTHONY LEWIS, JR.

Foreword

I love to make things complicated. It never seems like that while I'm in the middle of whatever the task is, but I truly *must* love it.

For years, I'd see a project and make a boulevard out of what only needed to be a single paved brick. And whenever it happened, an odd shape would knit my brow. At the same time, I wondered in frustration, what haunted motivation propelled me so deeply into business, with no desire to complete the task before me.

#startghetto

For context, I'm an artist. I'm pretty awesome at what I do, and I'm grateful for knowing that. I'm more thankful for knowing that before verbal and written validations from others. It's pretty dope. I rarely finish the things that I start, though. I tell myself:

I'm "trusting the process." I simply cannot "rush art."

Mostly though, it's just my archenemies: perfectionism. I allow it to control my successes. Yes, monetary gain is a success but, in most cases, just finishing something is my real mark of victory. I give those victories to perfection.

When La Tetra asked me to write these words you're reading now, I needed it to be so perfect, I didn't even start writing. For weeks, I deliberated, weighing impacts from messages I could give to her readers that would not only speak truth to them but embody her greatness?

And now, here we are, talking about finishing things. In a book titled, 'Start Ghetto.'

Perfectionism, folks. What an annoying dick.

From the moment she let us in on her internal dialogue, I was both shook and galvanized. Conversing with herself – in front of the world – Tee-Tee calls out demons not so different from mine. She sees her success, knows its flavor. She knows the only thing stopping her from attaining it is inaction.

I recognized this inner dialogue because I've had that very same conversation so many times before. But externally. Whenever people would ask about a thing that I did finish, I'd jump into motivational speaker mode, encouraging them to adopt a mindset of duplication:

"You don't have to be me to do what I did. You don't have to have whatever you think I have in order to even start. Hell, I don't even have half of what you think I do that even allowed me to get to the spot you see me standing in. Work with what you have."

It's taken years for me to have that same conversation with myself in the way that La Tetra will have with you. Partly because most of my whole life has been ghetto. And partly because once I got a taste of success, I put all my energy toward becoming all antithesis.

So, what am I saying? I'm saying honestly, **you've already read this book cover to cover, just by holding a space for its title in your mind.**

START GHETTO

Start ghetto. But start. And then finish. Don't rinse (because all the good flavor's in that pot) but definitely repeat.

Before you know it, you'll be just as insane as La Tetra and me, talking to yourself. But you'll have completed so much by then.

- Philip Anthony Lewis Jr., a chronic procrastinator.

#startghetto

PREFACE

THE TEA

Preface

The Tea

Aight. So, boom.

Let me tell you the real reason I wrote this book for you. Praise. Duh. No, but seriously. Have you ever been smacked with an idea and thought, "This one. *DIS DA ONE!*" as it danced around in your head? That was me a few weeks ago when I set out to write the most **traNsforMativE boOk eVeR**. I was ready and willing to serve you your life on a well-written platter, okay?! You were gonna get this lesson, baby! Two thoroughly flushed out parts and six chapters later, though, I threw it all in the trash.

The book I was writing started to feel a little too preachy. I shared information in a way that was above my pay grade. I began to unjustly scrutinize you and idealize the solutions to your problems. All of this in someone else's voice. I didn't know that woman *or* her voice.

As a writer, who has admittedly never finished reading a self-help book on this topic, I quickly realized why I would never finish writing my own if I didn't change something fast. *These types of books — as well-intended as they are — make me feel like shit.* When I'd pick one up to broaden my horizons, I'd put it down thinking, "I've been doing this shit all wrong." I leave wondering why I never seem to have the impossible prerequisites to getting my shit together enough to complete the easy-to-follow, step-by-step instructions. Once I realized I could potentially make my own readers feel like that, I trashed the whole document – minus my favorite part about discovering and leaning into your own nature.

Sometimes we orchestrate our own impostor syndrome by being actual impostors. Ironically, I was writing *Start Ghetto* against *my* own nature. I was forcing myself to fit the description of this person I made up so you wouldn't think I was so… me. I was writing as though I had all the answers for all the people. I almost missed the point. The point here is to meet each other as our most authentic selves.

I don't have all the answers for everyone. In fact, I have only been able to do what I have done and create the things that I've created because I know how to "do me" really well. I promised myself a long time ago that I would never create something that I wouldn't use or give advice that I wouldn't take. I will not start speaking with another tongue or dishonor my own promise just to write this book.

With that said, this book will contain a lot of colloquial phrasing because that's how I speak to my clients, family, friends, and myself. I am showing up as I am at this moment as to not contradict everything I will share in this text. Feel right at home in my candor and clumsiness. Be it some dry humor, tough love, or a little of the "*i*" word (inspiration), I hope you leave with what you came for.

- *La Tetra O.*

START GHETTO

#startghetto

CHAPTER 1

LET'S PRE-GIN

Chapter 1

Let's Pre-gin

Our ghettos are the odds we tell ourselves we have to beat before we're allowed to experience success. If no one ever told you this, I'll be the first:

Big Idea
You deserve and can absolutely aspire to, work for, and earn success even if you don't beat your odds or escape your ghetto.

Why am I calling your life ghetto? Isn't that word — that idea — offensive? Derogatory? Belittling? I mean...perhaps. If that is how you feel about being in or of the ghetto, I'm not here to convince you otherwise. However, for the purposes of **this** text, **ghetto** is the all-encompassing term for any physical, mental, or emotional space in which you feel restricted, stuck, and unable to make purpose-driven progress (as opposed to making progress for progress's sake).

I've also chosen to use the word 'ghetto' to double down on reaching people who believe they have to do things *against the odds*. It is time to change that narrative. When you do something against the odds, you are already accepting that there is a very low probability that it will happen. You are admitting that the desired outcome is unlikely.

When you think this way — when you choose to work *against* your environment and yourself, you raise your chances of not getting precisely what you want. You've already given yourself permission to not achieve because:
"At least I tried. I made it further than most people would in my situation. The odds were not in my favor."

Your ghetto is the existence of one or more circumstances that you cite when excusing yourself from creating goals and pursuing your version of greatness.

"I can't do this because…"
"I will do this when…"
"There is not enough ______ to…"
"Once I ______, then I can ______."

Whether or not they are self-created or forced upon you, your ghettos are self-defined. Even when we find ourselves in situations and with lifestyles that aren't ideal, it is still our own responsibility to press toward the fulfillment we claim we're seeking. You will usually find that the time you spent allowing your circumstances to hold you back *is* **the real** ghetto.

> **Street Smarts**
> Ghetto: the all-encompassing term for any physical, mental, or emotional space in which you feel restricted, stuck, and unable to make purpose-driven progress.

Sitting in Your Ghetto

Only you can decide that this is not the right time, place, or circumstance to start or continue "the thing." We all have our own ideas of how life should be and how much better life *will* be once this or that happens *for* us and things stop happening *to* us. Someone will always have it better than you. Just as you may covet the lives of others, there are some people who may look at your lot as the perfect set of conditions to thrive. However, you will never fully understand who is suffering in the same circumstances you feel you could succeed in and vice versa, **so don't obsess over it.**

In this book, I will share some of my own ghettos with you. Though you may be tempted to compare my circumstances to your own, don't. We are not here to compete in the struggle Olympics. When it comes to taking steps toward our goals, none of us have it easier than the next person because we all experience uniquely valid hardships. Identifying your hardships, though, does not relieve you of any responsibility in seeking fulfillment because no one can go after your desires for you.

Big Idea

It is important that we refrain from being chased out of our circumstances and learn to thrive in them.

Thrive. Hard stop. Not "until we can do better" or "for now," but with the acceptance that the things around you may or may not improve right away or ever. Still, you are responsible for making shit happen for yourself. Sit in your ghetto. Get to know it well.

Reflect + Check

What is it that you don't like about this place, and how you exist within it?

Street Smarts
The Thing: A specific, strong, and personal desired outcome.

But...I Hate It Here

Or you just feel *meh* about it. **Meh** is such a tight spot to navigate because you're alive and conscious. Yes, but you (or some part of you) exist on the autopilot which is disenchantment. Sometimes hate and lack of interest and enthusiasm can feel the same and yield the same outcome. Despite the obstacle in your way, you've held on to the possibility of making the thing happen for yourself. I know that because you picked up this book. I can tell because every time I say, "get started" or "the thing," you picture it (whatever it is). You know exactly what I'm referring to, and your body responds to just the idea of it.

Reflect + Check
Call it by name. Whatever it is that made your tummy rumble when you read "the thing," name it. When you bit your lip in nervousness when I said, "get started," what did you see? Say it out loud. Claim it for yourself. Don't hesitate. Whatever comes to mind right now, say it (even if you attract some stares on the train headed home from work).

Whether you have been dying to start eating plant-based, are putting off starting a business, or stalling on something I can't even imagine. Somewhere along the way, you've allowed hating or feeling meh about your not-good-enough circumstances to block you from getting exactly what you want.

Shit has just been much too ghetto for you to entertain your dreams, right? Too broke? Too fat? Living in the basement? Spouse can't get right? Yo' mama don't believe in you? Pencil ain't sharp enough? I've been there.

In the back of your mind, in the pit of your belly, or maybe even on the tip of your tongue exists the name(s) of exactly what you want. But everything you do suggests that *"maybe I don't deserve that level of fulfillment just yet."*

For many of us, there exists this idea that we need to be on the other side of our **unfortunate nows** to start setting and entertaining our deepest desires. But feeling more settled, having more resources, more education, fewer obstacles, and less fear will not decrease your desire to be further along in life.

We are human. We are always looking for more comfortable, fixed, figured out places and times to hunker down and start the real work. We have one deep desire that supersedes all of the others, though. **We want to avoid the bumps and bruises of hardship.** No one wakes up, stretches, and thinks, "I'm ready for a long hard day of struggle and discomfort!" No one. That is because we understandably aim to skirt discomfort and challenges; in many cases cheating ourselves out of many valuable lessons along the way. In this same avoidance, we miss opportunities to familiarize ourselves with our true nature. As a result, some of us will never learn who we are, what we want, or what we can achieve when we shoot our shots at our *actual* goals while our circumstances are less than favorable.

Street Smarts
Meh: Expressing a lack of interest or enthusiasm.
Unfortunate Nows: Moments of ambiguous hardship.

If you're still hollering, "But I hate it here," you should know that you will probably hate it wherever you think *there* is, too.

Big Idea
New circumstances do not guarantee a new you.

Who we are when the chips are down is exactly who we will be when the decks are stacked in our favor? It is paramount, then, that we put time and effort into discovering and leaning into our own nature to navigate external forces (however unpleasant they are).

The ghetto is everywhere. If you are not willing to at least try to thrive in this particular ghetto — the one you are in right now — you will not thrive in the ghettos to come; and you will never truly be able to establish and pursue the goals that are rooted in your deepest desires. **Ouch.** We will explore all of this in the coming chapters.

It Is What It Is, Friend

Many of us have fallen into the trap of taking advice about getting started from authors who do not truly speak directly to us, but over and around us. Maybe you've experienced this? If you have, it is important that I share my outlook on the modern usage of 'start where you are with what you have' rhetoric. It doesn't apply to all of us. This advice often lacks nuance and is not offered with where *you* are and what *you* have in mind. This call to action does not apply to those of us who are repeatedly smacked in the face with the realization that *where they are* is the fuck terrible and *what they have* is roaches (if you know, you know). This movement dismisses certain circumstances because some things are simply too uncomfortable to address.

Shit is not sugar! Some hardships cannot be romanticized. Some growth is ugly. Some feelings of lack are caused by actual scarcity and not just a scarcity mindset. It is unfortunate that some of us have been gaslighted into believing that we have enough to actually **start** where we are and make all of our wildest dreams come true. When we cannot imagine our own success, we are told to stop being negative. We are told that if we don't have "it" already we probably didn't want it in the first place. We get these messages in lazy, irresponsible sentiments like:

- You have the same number of hours in a day as Beyoncé.
- Failure is not an option!
- Things could always be worse.
- Everything happens for a reason.
- And other toxic bullshit dressed up as positive, superior thinking.

For me, these statements have always represented the casual abuse I've endured when I turned to self-help texts like this one in the past.

START GHETTO

"Start where you are with what you have" is only partially useful advice. It is vague. It tries to speak to everyone (with complete disregard of socioeconomic status, education level, physical ability, etc.) and reaches no one (really).

Big Idea

Start Ghetto is a charge. It requires you to manually pinpoint where you are and take inventory of what you have instead of ignoring the unpretty parts about your life in the name of automatic growth and forward movement. This command forces us to acknowledge the *not-okayness* of our situations so that we can strategically and practically address our real issues with getting started.

When we take the half-advice of starting where we are with what we have, we are led to believe that we are innately competent and well-enough equipped to complete and/or procure the thing. This is empowerment in a nutshell. But empowerment leaves with the person who empowered you when you look to them for more inspiration than instruction. It was a long, hard-learned lesson, but I eventually accepted that inspiration alone does not equal instruction. I needed both.

On the other side of this lesson, I can no longer encourage, support, or recommend the positive bullying that perpetuates our delusional thinking, shame, and the inevitable disappointment they breed. You do not have the same number of hours in your day as your favorite celebrity; and failure is not only an option, but a definite possibility.

You do not get to float out of your ghetto just because someone said a few inspirational words to you that one time in that one book. You must go through your shit; and even after you go through it, things may only get a little better. Be willing to acknowledge and sit in your ghetto for as long as you have to because things don't always change as quickly and as drastically as we feel they should. Strap in, and remember that:

Big Idea
Finding better circumstances is not the goal. The thing you want is the goal.

Your current circumstances are what they are until they aren't. What you do between here and there — now and then — is more up to you than you think.

You must go after the things you want even if your 24 hours feel like 10; and you must accept failure as a possibility because you'll likely fail a few times before, during, and after you see any progress. In order to take real steps toward actual accomplishments (and not just steps away from your hardships), you must first stop being your own foil.

In the next section, we will explore one of the most powerful "F" words working against you in your uphill battle to "just start" the way many self-help gurus recommend.

Finally:

The "Finally" Foil

"If I could just (get out of my current situation), I could **finally** ________ *."*

Like you, I've echoed some version of this phrase. Right before I entered adulthood (maybe even earlier), I spiraled into a perpetual desire to be further along than I was. Even when I did get to a "better place," my self-manufactured pang to be in an *even better* place never seemed to subside; and my qualifications for what was better became more elaborate. This would be true for me well into my twenties.

Even though I seemed to be hitting marks that signified my matriculation through adulthood, I was perpetually dissatisfied. Yes. I eventually got the jobs, but then I needed to save the money. I saved a little money, then I needed to move out on my own. Then pay all the bills. Then get out of debt. Each time I "arrived," I immediately began imagining how much better my life would be once I was just a few steps ahead. I always found a way to convince myself that it was neither the right time nor the right space to explore my aspirations to do or have *the things* because I was not where I thought I should have been in life.

I would fantasize about how I would finally be able to get serious about all of the things I wanted to do once I got my shit together; and instead of acting on these fantasies, I busied myself with chasing new circumstances in which I felt I would finally be able to entertain my dreams. Surely a new job would give me the security I needed to set goals. More commas in my savings account would help me build the confidence to take the first steps toward fulfillment. I would have all of the space and freedom I needed to create and work my master plan once I moved out on my own. This thought pattern followed me to every new circumstance.

Getting to the next circumstance *became* the goal. While I was laser-focused on the pursuit of better, I had never been further away from actual achievement. I tricked myself into thinking that a better set of circumstances was an achievement. I became the textbook definition of "hustle porn." I appeared booked and busy, but nothing I was doing was indicative of what I wanted from life.

I was in the thick of extreme burnout when I realized I wasn't actually accomplishing anything; just hopping from situation to situation waiting for the time to be just right for me to explore my passions. My eventual burnout did not come from setting and crushing goals, but from chasing a comfortable spot to do so. Imagine being dog-tired and feeling like you have nothing of real value to show for it.

I got the job and hated the boss. I saved the money, but I needed to use it to move. I moved out on my own and hustled to pay every bill. At each level of "success," I found myself screaming, "I hate it here."

How, Sway? These were the things I couldn't wait to have and the places I couldn't wait to go. These were the "ideal" situations that I wanted to be in before I started "the thing." I would eventually realize that the better circumstances of tomorrow came with an entirely new set of obstacles. These obstacles represented yet another gaggle of excuses I would use to play in the faces of my actual vision. Each new circumstance was its own sadistically contrived ghetto.

Hating from the Hallway

START GHETTO

I used to be completely mystified by people who had the ability to put something where nothing once was. I admired and secretly envied people who set out to do things with grace and finesse. I had convinced myself that these people were more special, more talented, and more creative than myself. At the very least they had more time and resources, right? How did they escape the rat race? How did they take a break from actual life to pursue their dreams? Where did they find the time? The audacity? Who gave them permission? Who was footing the bill?

My own frustration drove me to ~~study~~ hate-watch people who achieved things that I wanted to do. Each time, as if on cue, I was able to come up with a reason why they were able to accomplish great things while I was still looking for an "in" to the *Secret Society of Successful People* (it's not a thing. Don't Google it).

After a closer look, I noticed that this impenetrable collective of greatness was too diverse for me to put my finger on what made its members so great. The subjects of my hate-watching were both extremely wealthy and cash poor. They were both well-known and nameless. They lived both extravagantly and modestly. And then there was me – an outsider with my face pressed against the glass, minding other people's business, and still unable to find the resources necessary to mind my own.

Are You Minding Your Business?

The easiest way to stop being a hater is to mind your own business. You don't know how or why people have what they have, so stop concerning yourself with it because knowing won't bring you any closer to your thing. Just in case your mind still goes to that covetous place, you should know that even the most sought-after lifestyles have their difficulties. Some of your favorite public figures and private people with public lives – with all of their money, cars, and slowly-released vacation photos – are living all types of ghetto. This is why I insist that no matter how good you think you'd have it in someone else's performed existence, you should keep in mind that every observable lifestyle has its own set of ghettos for each unique person.

Our new, more pseudo-social world is one of exhibitionism and extremes. We are able to see people's highest highs without even asking for them. We are bombarded with highlight reels and prettified fails. Shit. As real as I want to be in this book, I will still attempt to make my failures look somewhat sexy. This is why I will repeatedly urge you not to compare your situations to the people mentioned here or in any other text, but to use these accounts as real-life examples of what may or may not work for you in your self-work.

Why Am I Telling You All of This?

I am not embarrassed to say that I have been that hater in the hallway. *Just as covetous as I wanted to be*. I am admitting my own problematic envy and exposing myself to you in this way because I understand the hopelessness and loneliness that comes with watching people "effortlessly":

1. discover and make room for their passions
2. set goals, and

3. pursue them with unbelievable success.

These glow-ups were especially hard to watch from my own personal slums. I wasn't going to just let it go. I was dying to:

1. know what these people knew that I didn't and
2. get to the bottom of my inability to live a life that aligned with my deepest desires.

After much sleuthing, I figured out that these people knew that if they ignored, pushed aside, or silenced their desire to do "the thing," every moment they spent not doing it would hurt like hell. They knew that their dream deferred would become a dull pain until they barely even noticed it.

They knew that it would eventually die. Okay. That was dramatic, but you get it; and I'm sure you've felt this exact twinge at some point. I have.

Before you begin fogging up some poor person's window with envy breath, I want you to understand that you do not have to be further along or a few more steps ahead of where you are right now to do a damned thing. You just have to be on *your* path. The right time, place, or circumstances to pivot to that path will never come for many of us so we have to be willing to "make something shake" right here and right now. Not out of desperation, but with the same vigor, entitlement, audacity, and perceived ease of the people we Stan.

But First, Accept These Things

1. At any given moment, you are where and how you are. There is only this and past versions of you. You can fantasize about your future self, their lifestyle, their finances, their level of education, but they have never existed and simply do not exist yet. With that in mind, it is cruel to project on them the results you are not willing to work for right now.

2. The things you do today will determine the lives of future versions of you. Past versions of you have let their circumstances – their temporary ghettos – put you in the ghetto you're in today. Aren't you fed up? Don't you wish that someone took action toward your goals sooner? How deep into "the

thing" would you be if just one version of you used their circumstances as tools of materialization instead of viewing them as prisons from which to be escaped?

3. Your circumstances can become a cage when you believe that in order to start making strides toward the things you SAY you want; you must escape something first. Once you decide that you need to transcend your situation before you can finally honor your desires and answer your callings, everything connected to that circumstance becomes a cell.

4. Finally, dreaming and pursuing your dreams is not a fucking luxury. You deserve to acknowledge your gut-

deep desires and carve out paths that lead to the things you named earlier in this chapter. Period.

What You'll Learn

In this book, you will learn to use your circumstances, unfortunate situations, and less-than-favorable conditions as tools. You will begin to use your now – however ghetto – as a growth mechanism rather than a contraption of doom. Through this text, you will create, fortify, and begin to use the self-talk required to pursue your goals *anyway* (whatever "anyway" means to you right now).

While reading, you will be prompted to complete various tasks that will assist you in curating your own self-supporting beliefs and practice behaviors that align with your true nature.

Big Idea

This text exists to help you move enthusiastically towards your wildest dreams; shamelessly and unapologetically as yourself; even when there are people who think you should not or cannot (and even if that person is you).

What This Philosophy Has Done for Me

Start Ghetto. This way of thinking has been that little extra oomph — that top-off of fuel — that energized me through creating new behaviors and realities while sitting firmly in my preexisting truths. It has made room for attitudes that help me dissolve envy, confront fear, and cancel my contracts with excuse-making. With these tools, I have been able to sprint towards my dreams instead of trying to outrun my circumstances.

This book is about unbinding ourselves from our obsession with opting into unnecessary rat races in our own avoidance of our big, scary desires. You will be challenged to redirect the motivation you already possess from **meantime measures** to shit you actually want to and should be doing.

At some point in your childhood you may have heard an authority figure say something like:

> *"If you spent as much time learning that (insert skill) as you did (insert waste of time activity), you probably would be better at (insert desirable activity)."*

As triggering as that reminder may be, the same sentiment still applies at your big age. If you spent as much time working toward your innermost desires instead of running from the potential discomfort of starting without the fancy prerequisites, you probably would be making significant strides toward "the thing."

If you want to keep waiting to reach a certain status to start *the thing*, put this book down. It is not for you. You can also skip this one if you enjoy being shamed into success. It's a real thing, so no judgment here. Finally, do not continue reading if you have the previously mentioned subjects all figured out. I would hate to bore you. Keep reading if:

1. you are tired of feeling like you must first reach a certain level of fame, fortune, or figure before

you name and honor your desires,

2. you want to learn how to fearlessly set realistic goals, and

3. you want to adopt and create self-supporting beliefs and behaviors that are unique to you and your true nature.

Who are you and what are you capable of when you are not running from something unattractive, but deliberately toward something sublime? What are your long- and short-term goals? What is your true nature?

Street Smarts

Meantime Measures: The things we do while waiting to do the things we want to do.

How To Use This Book

Throughout this text, you will find various prompts, calls-to-action, and activities. Don't ignore them. This guidebook includes interactive components that have been developed for easy navigation and comprehension. Look out for the following titles to enhance your understanding and application of topics covered in this text.

Big Ideas
The most important points are highlighted here.

Street Smarts

Useful terms are defined here.

Discovery

You will find various exercises and prompts here. These activities were created to help you ask the questions you typically wouldn't ask yourself without being provoked. The activities are simple and designed to do in a few minutes (sometimes seconds) as many times as you desire. They consist of some of the same questions I ask myself to stay in check. Make a habit of checking yourself. Eventually, it will become second nature (if it isn't already). For your own sake, be as honest as possible when completing the activities. If you are giving this book a re-read, note how your responses differ from read to read.

These activities include:

1. Write It Out

Keep paper or a journal handy to answer questions asked throughout the text.

2. Reflect + Check

No materials needed. Just bring your memories and an open mind.

3. A Closer Look

Explore your reflections deeper.

As mentioned in **Write it Out**, keep a journal handy so that you can reflect on your past answers as often as needed. Feel free to customize the activities — formally while reading this text and informally while experiencing life.

While this book flows from cover to cover, each passage is written to be understood on its own. You can read chapters, sections, and parts that jump out at you if you wish to quickly gather or regather your life.

This book is full of nuggets and gems in the form of first and secondhand examples. I ask that wherever possible, you do not compare your life to my own or the lives of others I may mention in this text. Instead, apply the principles and lessons learned to your unique situations for the very best use of the material.

Do not force yourself to power through this book. Getting through the material quickly is not the goal here. Put it down and pick it up as you see fit. Question it. If something doesn't make sense, disregard it or rip out the problematic page and show it to your therapist. Remember that I am just another person with a coaching certification that you found on Michelle Obama's Internet. There is always room for a second, third, and 15th opinion.

At the end of each chapter, look for the bulleted chapter summary under **Basically…** where the main take-aways from each chapter have been consolidated. Immediately following the chapter summary, you will find a sneak peek of the next chapter.

Basically…

- You deserve and can absolutely aspire to, work for, and earn success even if you don't beat your odds or escape your ghetto.
- It is important that we refrain from being scared out of our ghettos and learn to thrive in them.
- New circumstances do not guarantee a new you.
- *Start Ghetto* is a charge. It requires you to manually pinpoint where you are and take inventory of what you have instead of ignoring the unpretty parts about your life in the name of automatic growth and forward movement.
- Finding better circumstances is not the goal. The thing you want is the goal.

- It is important that we refrain from being scared out of our ghettos and learn to thrive in them.
- DO NOT COMPARE YOURSELF!

In the next chapter, we will discuss some reasons why you haven't set goals, haven't set the right goals, or have set weak goals.

START GHETTO

#startghetto

CHAPTER 2

YOU ARE HERE

Chapter 2
You Are Here

You Have A Goal Setting Issue

No lead-burying here. I've decided to *start* discussing goal setting at this point so that you can consume the rest of this text with goal development and some necessary reassurance fresh on your mind.

Big Idea

Sometimes we think we are failing at our goals, not realizing that we haven't actually set any.

Yes. We all want things, so someone telling you you don't have any goals may sound a little problematic to you. But having things that you want to accomplish does not mean that you've set goals for any of it. This chapter will help you understand and address why you haven't set goals. Believe it or not, there are valid reasons why someone who wants to set goals would feel like they never can. If you are a goal-setting master, skip this chapter. If you are still working to be better at goal setting, pay close attention here.

Still reading? Yes? Then you probably agree that goals give us the momentum to push through adversity while chasing our dreams. You know that you should set goals to help you to achieve your aims and objectives, but you haven't. Why? The concept of goal setting is not new to you. You are familiar with the studies that prove that setting and writing specific, measurable, attainable, relevant, and timed goals are necessary and effective. You could probably teach all about **SMART** goals and you may have recommended it to a few of your peers.

Perhaps you loosely know what your goals are but have told yourself that you don't have the time to sit down and write them out on real paper with real ink. If you have all of this knowledge but truly don't have the time, put **this book down right now** and use the minutes you would have spent reading this section to get those goals onto a piece of paper.

Still reading? Great. You have time, then. **Let me holla at you real quick** about why you may not be setting those goals. I am absolutely certain that if you have made it this far in this text, lack of time is not your problem. In the sections to follow, we will uncover some common reasons you aren't setting goals. Please note that you may identify with a different reason (or set of reasons) with each read. You may also have reasons not listed here. Be sure to add them to your journal for reference.

Street Smarts
SMART: An acronym that stands for Specific, Measurable, Attainable/Achievable, Relevant/Realistic, and Timely in reference to goals.

Reason 1. I Don't Believe It

You've read the goal setting tips but can't see it working for you. You understand why and how setting goals work, you are just not fully convinced that setting goals will further your cause. This skepticism can sometimes creep up on us when we haven't seen our potential goals set or reached by people like us who we have or can gain access to.

Write It Out

Do I have access to people of similar backgrounds and/or circumstances that have set or completed similar goals? If not, can I gain that access? If I do, do I intentionally surround myself with those people?

My brother who is nine years younger than I wanted to be a fire truck. When I explained to him that he could not be a fire truck, he listed all the great qualities of the truck and it made perfect sense to me why he thought he could be one.

As children, many of us didn't learn how to intentionally pick our **role models.** We learned that we should have them, and we learned why. Yet somehow it was missed that a role model can be situational. People who are well-behaved, high-earning, and generous are likely the role models we were told we should have. Teachers, parents, civil servants, and firetrucks all represent noble, humble, and generic characters to aspire to. They are admirable.

Maybe you're still picking role models this way. Are you still choosing role models that are socially acceptable? Popular? Noble? The older we get, the more ineffective this method becomes. Just because someone (or in my brother's case something) is admirable, doesn't mean they are meant to lead the way. While the person or people you admire may be *someone's* role model, maybe they aren't yours. Just because someone is impressive and worthy of your respect, doesn't necessarily mean they are the appropriate people to emulate in all areas of life.

Young or old, we get to choose our role models. We must. It is important that we choose them carefully. This requires us to get specific about the areas of our lives in which we need representation and assistance to get from point A to point B. We need to see that the thing we want is achievable. This requires us to know exactly what that thing is.

Even after picking more specific role models, we can still be tricked into not believing that our potential goals can happen for us because we have picked the wrong person/ people to emulate.

Big Idea
Sometimes, we pick the wrong role models; causing us to fall short of our goals or discouraging us from setting the goals in the first place.

Do you find yourself attracted to those who are living the best version of your desired life? Maybe it's time to take a closer look at your *faves* glow-up. With careful consideration, you may find that while your role model is AMAZING, they did not take a path to your potential goal that you can emulate. Trying to emulate someone who started with certain advantages can eventually cause us to view the things we want as things we can't get.

Be honest. How many times have you found yourself shying away from certain aspirations because you were looking up to people who did it rich as fuck, in a better environment, or maybe even with better looks?

I am not calling you poor or ugly; and I am certainly not telling you to exclusively surround yourself with or look up to broke, ugly folk. What I *am* saying is that you will find and keep better role models when you stop overlooking your struggle mates.

People who have been through what we've been through are the best at modeling our possible next steps on our own journeys because they are likely to have experienced similar obstacles and ease. When I was trying to go vegan (the first time) I wanted to learn from the most vegan-est vegans. I followed all of these middle class, life-long vegans who lived off their land and only ate cooked foods on special occasions. After falling short of a vegan lifestyle several times, I realized that I should have been sitting at the feet of people who had similar access to food sources and a relatable funding situation to pay for that food. My journey became a lot easier once I started learning from people who weren't born into veganism and those who were still learning themselves. *These* were my role models.

Through choosing or having limited access to the wrong role models, we can perpetuate our own skepticism about goal attainability. Unfortunately, this skepticism can keep us **GOALLESS**. We use this skepticism to strengthen our claim that certain things just won't work out for us. But, is it possible that you look down on the same people that are **evidence** that a person like you could succeed at the thing? They are the proof you need to put your skepticism to rest. Perhaps your inability to accept where *you* are maybe causing you to snub people who could help you carve a *realistic* path to meeting your goals.

Many of our faves who have time, money, or even genetics on their side usually find effortlessness in our most arduous journeys. This is why it is hard to connect with their success even when we want it so badly.

Reflect + Check

Am I skeptical about my ability to achieve? If skepticism is my reason for not setting goals, what have I done to contribute to my own disbelief? How will I work towards finding more of the role models I need and less of the ones I want?

Street Smarts
Role Model: A person looked to by others as an example to be imitated.

Don't ignore your struggle mates. No one wants to struggle to the finish line, but we can look to the people who have to help us get real about the road ahead of us. From people who did the thing under similar circumstances, we can learn what to avoid, what to do better, and how to get there faster.

Reason 2. I'm Afraid to Fail

Another reason why you may not be setting goals is fear. Our fear can sometimes lead to long periods of inaction. We are often advised to 'do it scared.' But those of us who have experienced fear paralysis know that we don't always get that surge of adrenaline we need when faced with a big, scary dream. It is easy to enter a loop of doing the same things we have always done like:

- setting the wrong goals and
- misusing our comfort zones

Sometimes we are afraid that our goal is too big and that we will not be able to make it happen. We are afraid of the hurt and embarrassment that comes with failure. Maybe you are afraid that people like you just cannot be THAT fortunate.

How many times have you downgraded your desire once someone asked you to get specific? Our fears can come in the form of settling for the next best thing. I once asked a mentee who expressed to me that she wanted to lose weight about how much weight she wanted to lose. She excitedly gushed about wanting to lose 50 lbs, the clothes she would wear once she did, etc. But when I asked her to set a goal to get there, she suddenly became okay with 25-30 lbs. and became less excited about her '*dream bawdy*' as she called it. It appeared that suddenly her goal of losing 50 lbs seemed ridiculous once she was asked about her plan to get there. My question triggered panic and my mentee clung to an old goal she knew she could meet because she had met it before.

Reflect + Check
Am I allowing fear to talk me out of my desire to ______?

A Closer Look
What is the fear? The pain of past failures? Potential embarrassment?

Write It Out
What current obstacles exist because of my fear of failure? How will failure continue to disrupt my life?

Once we are able to understand the source of our fears, we can begin to rebuild our excitement about our original desire and confidently set the appropriate goal(s).

Big Idea
The reason why some people actually fail is because they are afraid to fail.

And what do you do when you are afraid to fail? You either don't start at all or you consciously or subconsciously make half-assed attempts. We don't have to do this to ourselves anymore. Moving forward, we are no longer bracing for impact in anticipation of punches that may not ever come.

When we say we are afraid to fail, what we are actually saying is, "I'm not good enough," while simultaneously convincing ourselves that our mistakes are life-ending. You have to be willing to look silly. Sometimes, that looks like dealing with your beliefs about what is embarrassing so that you can confidently make your mistakes, learn from them, and go about your business.

All failure isn't *bad* failure. The first time I heard that I was BLOWN away, but I understood it immediately as it was knowledge that I already had, but hadn't fully accepted. There are still times where I'll work really hard toward a specific goal only to have my plan thwarted by one thing or another. I've made a lot of missteps and have had plenty of doors closed in my face, but those "failures" sprouted new goals or helped me amend, reinforce, or go harder at my existing goal.

Failure helps us adjust the objectives, strategies, and tactics that aid in the completion of our goals. Our response to failure helps us weed out tolerable situations from our dreams. In the end, only our most worthy endeavors survive the devastation of failure. So it is better to fail sooner rather than later.

Through failure, I have had some of my most profound epiphanies. Failing has fed me ideas and put me in positions that I couldn't have even anticipated and didn't even know I wanted until I was confronted with them. Each time I have failed (and I have failed a lot) my goals have become more refined and enriched.

You will fail at tasks, you will fail missions, but you will never fail at a goal until you stop pursuing it. Each moment you spend afraid to set goals, you are already setting yourself up for the ultimate "L."

Reflect + Check

What role does fear play in my goal setting habits?

Write It Out

Write down a list of things you haven't done because of your feelings of inadequacy. These list items can be anything from finally drawing a picture on that canvas you bought to cutting a thirteen-song album in the voice memos of your phone. Put it out there.

Reason 3. I Did It Wrong Before

Did you know that you could set the wrong goals? We briefly touched on setting the wrong goals in Reason 2. Wrong is a strong word, right? But it really helps us understand why some of our older goals didn't click.

Remember that burnout I was talking about in the last chapter? Yeah. That came from driving really fast in the wrong lane. I was setting the goals that I thought I was supposed to set based on the beliefs, ideals, and desires of my family at home, teachers at school, and friends, acquaintances I would meet throughout my life, and my own ego. We go through this more often than we think. Sometimes we feel pressured to please, emulate, and feel closer to people that their goals become ours. Love and admiration can do that to you. The pair is so strong that they can cause us to believe that the goals of others (or the goals that we have been assigned by others) are the ones we've created for ourselves.

Other times, we allow our egos to be the driving force in the kind of goals we set. We choose goals that make us look good and ones that will elicit adoration.

Big Idea

Be careful not to set the wrong goals and know how to identify when you have.

I was so good at being successful at the wrong goals because it is easy to confuse what we are good at with what we want. Aptitude can be a trap. We will find a bunch of things we are good at while executing the wrong goals. The trick is not to get lulled into complacency by your abilities and other people's plans for them.

You will know when you are setting the wrong goals when:

1. **Achievement came too fast and easy.** Your goal should be sufficiently challenging and require more than minimal effort. It should stretch you in some way. That is why we set goals. We are not where we want to be, so we set the goal to get there. A goal that seems too easy to achieve was probably not your goal. Maybe it was a milestone in a journey to your real goal.

   Do not confuse this for making things hard for no reason but do try to pick a goal that is expansive to your life in some way.

2. **Completion is ambiguous.** You should never be confused about whether or not a goal has been completed. Your goal should be measurable, and the anticipated outcomes should be clearly defined. Be committed or table your goal because commitment to your goal is essential to goal completion. Set goals that you have a burning need to achieve that way you know exactly what achievement looks like for you. Share your goal with people that you trust and who are likely to support you for an extra pop of accountability.

3. **Execution causes you to be overwhelmed.** In many cases, the wrong goal can feel burdensome. Your goal may be out of your reach

because it was not your goal in the first place, or it should have been broken down into smaller goals that combine to produce one major outcome. While your goals should be expansive, they shouldn't wipe you out completely. Break down your goal as much as you have to even if it means that achievement will take a little longer.

4. **There were unforeseen negative consequences.** Sometimes we spend more time and money than expected on achieving what we think are our goals. If your pursuit of the goal causes significant pain to you or those important to you, you may need to revise or abandon that goal if it is the cause of unnecessary misfortune or greatly interfering

with preexisting goals, your health, or the well-being of your loved ones.

It isn't always worth it to 'do it scared.' Sometimes what we are told to brush off as baseless fear, is actually our intuition urging us to be mindful of the avoidable pitfalls. Our own carelessness or pride can cause us to miss the warning signs that certain paths are not meant for us. Be willing to stop and look into these fears. If you find that you need to make some changes, make them. It is okay to revise or abandon goals if you realize you've set the wrong goals or have the wrong motivations for completing a certain goal.

Big Idea

#startghetto

Whatever you do, don't let having done it wrong before stop you from setting new goals.

Reason 4. I'm Comfortable Here

Comfortable or not, you need to set new goals. That same comfy spot you are sitting in is a reminder that we grow into and out of things. Maybe you are experiencing your comfort at work or in your relationship. Maybe you are comfortable with your health or your financial habits. Do you remember how odd you felt when you first got to that spot? You had to do some growing to feel the comfort that you are feeling right now. Guess what. You are not going to stop growing. Eventually, you will outgrow this place, too.

Big Idea

Being comfortable where you are is not all bad. It is the

perfect place to set new goals for yourself.

Why wait until you've had enough of your current situation to take a huge, unnecessary leap of faith. Most people don't approach comfort zones this way. The discussion around them is that we have to get out of them in order to be successful. **Leap of faith**. That is only half true.

It can be tempting to cling on to our 'good place' especially when it is far better than where we came from. For many of us, getting outside of our comfort zone sounds really inconvenient. The truth is that one way or another, we WILL always get out of our comfort zones. None of us gets to stay there. It is from those same comfort zones, though, that we get to decide whether we want to gracefully emerge or be evicted without warning. If you could help it, would you wait for the last day of your lease to start looking for a new place to live? No. Then why would you choose to wait until you're super uncomfortable to set new goals? If you can help it, do not wait to outgrow your current comfort zone. Use the space and time that comfort allows you to set new goals and position yourself to work new plans.

Reason 5. I Want I Now, Though

Do you? Do ya really prefer microwave success? Impatience is one of the most counter-intuitive reasons to **not** set a goal. Would you rather your goal take a 'long time' or to never have it at all? Not setting a goal due to your impatience will ensure you the latter.

When one victory comes fast, we start to think that everything will come that way. Most progress, though, is slow and we fuel our own disappointment when we reject it for not being fast enough. Imagine you're cooking a chicken. The recipe calls for the chicken to bake for one hour, however, at the one hour mark your chicken was still raw in the middle. Would you throw the chicken out or would you keep the chicken in the oven a little longer? Some of us have picked up the unfortunate habit of throwing out our chicken when we feel it's cooking too slowly; not realizing that (1) recipes are only suggested guidelines and (2) slow is the default. You will never eat dinner if you keep throwing out the half-cooked chicken. Don't let impatience allow you to make decisions that don't make sense to the ultimate goal.

I am notorious for throwing out my chicken due to illogical impatience. This behavior shows up in full force particularly when my goal involves me saving money for something big. Once when I was saving to move, I reasoned with myself that it was okay to spend some of the money I had saved on something else since I had not saved all of the money as quickly as I had planned. Make that make sense. I would have never reached my goal savings if I kept using that logic. Not only did my impatience cause me to throw out my chicken, but it also caused me to settle for scrambled eggs EVEN THOUGH I STILL WANTED THAT CHICKEN.

Ultimately, our impatience impacts our ability to feel satisfied. When you want chicken, eggs just won't do the trick; and when you want a new apartment, a vacation won't do it either. Even though you like the feeling of touching SOMETHING as soon as possible, be clear that something will never be as tasty as *the* thing. Use slow progress to make room for new lessons that will strengthen your ability to navigate future goals (or cook future chickens).

Reflect + Check

Think about some things in your life that came quick and easy. Maybe it was last night's dinner. Maybe it was a relationship (oop). Maybe it was a job you chose over another because it came easier than the one you really wanted. How are those things working out for you? Was it the best meal you ever had? Do you still rock with what's her/his name? Do you still want that other job?

Naturally, we want some things to come easy because that's just the way things are now. No judgment if you partake in fast fashion, food, and funding, but let it end there.

Big Idea
Don't let your need for instant gratification seep into the vision you have for your life.

The aim here is not to completely abandon your need for instant gratification, but to use it to your advantage. I recommend identifying **milestones** to everyone but especially the impatient. Being able to track our success through our milestones appeases that need for instant gratification that we all have to some degree.

An 'I want it now' mentality may not be the best way to set goals, but if that is where you are, use it. Working with your impatience can look like clapping for every little win while you are taking steps toward your goal. I used this exact advice to complete this book. This book was divided into multiple different documents. Each document contains a chapter. I've chosen to mark each complete chapter with a star upon completion. I have even gone as far as identifying milestones within each milestone. In doing this, I periodically satiate my need for instant gratification.

Street Smarts

START GHETTO

Milestone: An action or event marking a significant change or stage in development.

Reason 6. I've Been Hurt

Somewhere between childhood and today, you've learned how to protect yourself from potential disappointment. As children, we would naturally get back up and try again when we failed at walking, playing, learning to eat, etc. We all have people in our lives that tried to shield us from potential pain because they didn't want to see us in pain (or deal with the fallout of our disappointment). Ultimately, we've learned how to do this for ourselves. I get it.

Big Idea
Hanging onto previous disappointments can stop you from setting new goals.

Have you learned to manage your expectations instead of taking the necessary steps to recover from the disappointment of non-achievement? This could be the reason why you have set weak goals or haven't set any at all. There is nothing inherently wrong with wanting to avoid unnecessary pain, but some pain is not unnecessary. When we actively work toward recovery from our last disappointment, we can move forward in our goal setting with more tolerance for whatever future let-downs we may face.

Adults are not as resilient as children. We have to put effort into our own recovery. Here are some steps you can take to avoid letting disappointment lead.

1. **Allow your feelings.** You will not overcome disappointment by pretending you are not hurt.

Sometimes we cannot admit to our disappointment because we want to save face. You may have told yourself that you didn't want something anyway or that it wasn't your time, but you owe yourself more reflection and introspection than that.

2. **Acknowledge your unmet needs.** If you are disappointed because your needs were not met, examine what those unmet needs are so that you can work towards having your needs met next time.

3. **Invest in your bounce back.** This is where all of that self-care content you've been indulging in comes into play. You should

always aim to take the very best care of yourself but be a little more intentional and less robotic about how you go about caring for yourself after a disappointment. Do not count out actual therapy because sometimes disappointment is *that* serious.

4. **Examine your expectations.** Maybe you had unrealistic expectations of someone who was supposed to help you along. Maybe you had these expectations of yourself. Explore how you may have been complicit in your own disappointment. Use this information to express how you were let down. Start the conversation(s) so that your

expectations can be adjusted accordingly.

5. **Set boundaries if you need to.** Sometimes we let people's expectations of us get in the way of what we 'got goin' on over here!' Make a habit of setting clear boundaries for yourself. This may include not being financially available to someone who asks you for money too often when you have a financial goal. It can also include not being open to gossip or venting sessions from friends, family, and co-workers when you are working toward a spiritually charged goal.

Reason 7. I Lack the Energy

And that is fine because...don't we all. It is okay to admit that you don't have the energy to take on your goals at the moment.

Big Idea
Goals need to be backed by energy. Without the proper energy allotted to your goals, you're going to continue to half-step towards your goals.

Maybe you are reading this book because you are looking to redirect your energy from another area of your life to your goals.

Write It Out

Make a list of all the things that you do that you could afford to cut back on for the purposes of pursuing your goals. These things are usually trivial and mostly enjoyable. Order your list from most enjoyable to least enjoyable and try to eliminate the things you dislike the most first.

Maybe you'll find that you could watch less television or "get off that damn phone" (if you know, you know). This is not about deprivation. It is about really taking stock of how you spend your time and what you can make less important for the sake of bringing the proper energy to your gut-deep desires.

Set the goals that you really want — the ones that are really important to you. Bring that same energy that you exert on activities and thoughts that are not your goals to the things that are, and watch shit get done.

You probably aren't experiencing all of these roadblocks right now, but some of them will come up because...life. When they do, remember that you have been working on developing your own self-talk to better position yourself to set your next goal.

Basically…

- Have you failed at your goals or not set any?
- Don't perpetuate your own skepticism about the goals you want to set.
- Your fear of failure could be causing you to fail.
- Your comfort zone is the perfect place to set new goals.
- Don't let your need for instant gratification seep into the vision you have for your life.
- Hanging onto previous disappointments can stop you from setting goals.

In the next chapter, we will discuss how to identify, prioritize, and solidify your goals.

START GHETTO

#startghetto

CHAPTER 3

GET GOALSY

Chapter 3
Get Goalsy

Now that we've examined some reasons why you may not have set your goal and you've identified *your* specific reasons; you are prepared to Get Goalsy (it's like 'ballsy' but for goals) in this chapter. The truth is that setting my goals – even the smaller ones – has required big balls because I want big things that I haven't seen anyone like me complete. So, getting 'goalsy' is my way of remembering that goal setting is just as much of a process as achieving them. Here we will discuss:

- what actions to take before goal setting,
- how to identify what your goals are,
- the anatomy of a well-crafted goal, and
- how to prioritize and solidify your goals.

Roles Before Goals

Many of us have so much we want to accomplish in life. It can be hard to determine what comes first or what deserves/ requires more of our attention. Before we set any goals, we can easily narrow our scope by defining our roles in life. Some of my roles are entrepreneur, coach/mentor, and now an author. I am also an individual, daughter, sister, wanderlust, and more. Defining your roles forces you to look more holistically at your life in its entirety. Listing and acknowledging these roles has helped me mitigate the laser-like focus I tend to have as an entrepreneur. Even if you are not an entrepreneur, it is easy to become hyper-focused on one of our roles while neglecting others. Defining your roles forces you to think about your life holistically.

In defining our roles, we must consider who we are to ourselves as well as who we are to others. Your possible roles could include, but are not limited to:

- **Your familial status(es).** Mother, father, daughter, son, uncle, aunt, sibling, matriarch, etc.
- **Your employment status(es).** Employee, entrepreneur, coach,

founder, doctor, boss, community organizer, political figure, etc.

- **Your personally assigned status(es).** Truth teller, light seeker, adventurer, motivator, influencer, etc.

The list goes on.

Write It Out
Create a list of all the different roles you have in life.

Now that you've defined your roles. We can determine which of those roles take up the most time and which are most important. To add to your exercise, make two columns on a sheet of paper. In one column, list your roles according to how much time they take up or how much space they occupy in your life. In the second column, list your role based on their importance. Your lists can go from greatest to least or vice versa, as long as you choose the same option for both lists.

What Is A Goal?

Have one million liquid dollars in 365 days.

Just like that.

A goal is a brief, clear statement of an outcome to be reached within a specific timeframe. It is a broad, general, tangible, and descriptive statement. Your goal is measurable by quantity and quality. Your goal does not outline HOW something should or will be done, but just what the results will be. From the goal I have declared above, you can tell that by the end of 365 days, I will have one million dollars in cash money. My goal is:

1. **Broad + General.** This goal is broad and general because I did not specify how I would go about obtaining my 'milli.' Make sure you do not concern yourself with potential plans while setting your goal. We will discuss planning later.

2. **Tangible.** Not to be confused with 'material.' You should eventually be able to experience it with one of the senses. A tangible goal ensures that your goal is measurable and attainable. I will be able to see $1,000,000 across my bank accounts or touch the money in my hands.

3. **Descriptive.** If someone is reading your goal, they should be able to identify the who, what, when, and

where (when applicable). The goal above expresses the timeframe, the thing I want, and that I am the one that wants it. 'Where' is implied.

4. **Measurable by quality.** Liquid dollars. This means that I want to be able to have my money in cash or easily converted into cash. By specifying this, I am establishing the quality by which achievement of my goal is measured.

5. **Measurable by quantity.** $1,000,000. In goal setting, it is not sufficient to simply declare that you want money or enough money to *xyz*. Adding a quantity to your goal lets you know when you can stop working toward your goal and proceed with the necessary next steps.

Identify Your Goals

There are a few things you should understand about goals before we start setting them.

1. Your dreams and fantasies are important but are not equal to your goals.
2. Your goals are specific, desired results or targeted objectives.
3. A goal is something you can and should put your energy and effort behind to achieve it.
4. Despite your circumstances, you can get what you want if you set the right goals supported by a plan of action.

Many coaches, authors, and teachers in the goal-setting niche will often start here:

"Identify your interests. What makes you happy?"

But what if you don't know what those things are? What if you have not yet discovered the source of your happiness. Most text will assume that you have that figured out and are able to put it into words. Dried sweet mangos and cookies make me extremely happy but are irrelevant interests when it comes to the goals I'd like to set and have set in the past. So, it is important that we identify what kind of happiness we're talking about before we start using temporary states of being to solidify our goals.

I never start any goal setting session with 'what makes you happy?' because what makes you happy right now may not contribute to your happiness in the future. Yes, I enjoy sweet treats now, but will I enjoy them as much if several of my teeth have cavities or my digestive system can no longer handle the sugar? If you have ever stopped seeing the usefulness of completing your goal somewhere before it was completed (or even after), it is possible that you have hedonic responses to 'what makes you happy?'. Hedonic happiness demonstrates how our brief experiences of joy and pleasure can quickly fade away; undermining and potentially nullifying any goals we've made in that spirit. Enjoying sweets does not mean I should open a candy store. As obvious as that looks on paper, it has taken me years to understand that I do not have to turn everything I enjoy into work. Some things are meant to be experienced, enjoyed, and filed under things that give us pleasure.

Our experiences with this intense, fleeting happiness often overshadow our long-term satisfaction — eudemonic happiness. When asked, "what makes you happy?" it is easy to discount or under-emphasize the importance of our own general well-being because it is obvious that we want to be well. It really isn't that obvious, though, which is why we have to actively sort the things that contribute to our long-term well-being. For the purposes of goal setting, the most valuable answers to 'what makes you happy?' will usually become apparent to you when you make a habit of asking yourself, 'What do I want? What do I need?' and using the answers that you've compiled over time to discover which sources of happiness aid in your overall well-being and align with your true nature.

We can identify what we want and need by simultaneously considering our most important roles, areas that influence our lives, and our interests. So... What *do* you want? What do you need?

If you are having as much trouble identifying what contributes to your happiness as I once did, this section will help you. We will consider six areas of life that influence our gut-deep desires and contribute to our overall happiness and wellness. Through identifying these areas, we can further understand how to move forward in our goal setting.

When considering our eudemonic happiness, our main areas of influence from which most of our desires are born include:

1. Career
2. Financial
3. Health + fitness
4. Lifestyle
5. Relationships
6. Spirituality + religion

Write It Out

Based on the six listed areas of influence, which of your personal interests come to mind? Your personal interests can be experiences you've had and would like more of or some things you're curious about. You may find that some interests can be listed in more than one area of influence.

While these six areas combine to contribute to our overall state of being and help us categorize our roles and interests, they often conflict, making our ability to set the right goals that much more confusing. To add to the confusion, our temporary ideas about happiness can also conflict with the goals we may need to set.

Write It Out

Set one specific goal in each area that you'd like to accomplish within the next 12 months (we'll keep the timeframe short for now, but you can extend it if you need to). Your goal should be broad, general, tangible, descriptive, and measurable by quality and quantity. Perhaps your goals align with your interest. Maybe they don't. Maybe you will identify new interests while setting your goals.

Did you do the **Discovery** exercises? Did you set a goal in *every* area? Here is some advice for you if you didn't. *Your goals do not have to be profound to be worthy of pursuit.* If you left a section blank because your goal didn't feel 'big enough' that was for you. Your lifestyle goal can be as pragmatic as opening all of your mail once a week instead of letting it accumulate for months. For some of us, the 'big scary dream' is just that practical. Do not shy away from identifying something as a goal because it is "too practical" or "anyone can do it." If you need to do it, it can be a goal.

If you are still having trouble finding the words for your goal, ask yourself:

"How can my life improve in this area."

If you are honest with yourself, you can always find something to improve on even if it isn't glamorous or sexy. This exercise is not meant for you to nitpick at your life. It is meant to ensure that you are honoring your circumstances and prioritizing your needs in a way that adds to your ultimate well-being.

If you did not complete the exercise, go back and fill in the blanks. Also, take this time to go over the goals you have written down in each section. Don't overthink this. You may have multiple goals for each area but just focus on one for now (perhaps the one that inspired you to pick up this book).

Prioritizing Your Goals

As you've read in the last chapter, sometimes we think we need everything right now. This is not the case. If sitting in front of your six goals causes a bit of overwhelm or impatience, that is normal. Looking at that many life changes at once is alarming, but it is possible to dissolve some of that overwhelm if we figure out what our priorities are.

To start understanding where your priorities lie, make a list of three to five reasons why you want to accomplish each goal.

> **A Closer Look + Write it Out**
> Consider each goal separately. For every goal you've listed, create a list of your motivations for completing each goal. You can answer the following questions if you need help getting started with your lists.

1. Why is this goal important *right now*?
2. What *benefits* will I enjoy once I achieve this goal?

Once you are done, highlight three goals that make you feel excited or nervous. Use the motivations you've listed to help you. If your financial goal is to make $2,000 this month from your small business, does that evoke an emotion? Are you excited to have the money in your hand? Are you afraid you might miss the mark? Whichever three goals are the most evocative, let's focus on those.

Now that you are looking at your three main goals, pick the goal you want to focus on. There are two ways you can choose which goal you should pour in to.

1. **The most urgent.** Which of these goals is the most urgent? Which of them needs to happen right now?!
2. **The most helpful:** Which goal will help you complete other goals?

Use your own discernment to determine what is helpful.

After completing this exercise, you will start to understand the motivations behind your main goal. These are your '**whys**.' Your whys are what motivate you to solidify your goal and work your plan to completion. Your whys confirm that your goal is authentic to your desires and in alignment with your true nature. Your whys will help you figure out 'how'. Any goal without a why, then should be crossed off your list first, followed by goals with shallow whys.

Why do I want one million liquid dollars within the next 365 days? Financial freedom. Never being in debt again is one of my main motivations for collecting, saving, and growing these coins. For me, having a base of one million dollars at my disposal means I won't have to take out loans for future endeavors and I can continue doing the work I want without worrying about funding. I want to be able to live comfortably while I focus on making my next few millions. A shallow why for having one million dollars would be to stunt on all of you. Nobody would disagree that *coming into* that kind of money would be nice (or life-changing, even), but I increase my chances of holding it in my hands because I have set a goal for it. Now, I don't have to think about coming into it because I know that I am actively working towards it (but if a stranger wants to slide some my way, get in touch.)

If you've had trouble setting goals in the past, you know all too well how difficult it can be to stay the course. You are not an anomaly. Most goals reach some sort of opposition and resistance. Discovering your 'why' increases your chances of success even if you've experienced or are currently experiencing some of the hardships we discussed in chapter one. Our whys also help us pivot to the right goal when we find that we've set the wrong goal (as discussed in Chapter 2). With that in mind, understand that your whys — your motivations — are as important as the goals themselves.

Street Smarts

Whys: Reasons or motives that back your goals.

#startghetto

Basically…

- Make your goal a brief, clear statement of an outcome to be reached within a specific timeframe.
- Always back your goal with an important why.
- Prioritize your main goal by determining what is most urgent or what can help you take steps towards completing other goals.
- Understand that your goals may not always align with your interests.
- Check all of your goals against SMART for the best possible outcome.

In the next chapter, we will discuss planning for goal completion.

#startghetto

CHAPTER 4

GET PLANNY

Chapter 4

Get Planny

Planning is how we anticipate and manage our results to the best of our ability. It helps us figure out what actions should be taken to reach our goals as well as helps us determine how each action can impact subsequent actions.

Big Idea

Within our plan, we create guidelines and smaller goals that aid in our ultimate desired results.

It is here that we carve our own paths and create our own rules, so it is paramount that we are honest about what we believe we can do and how far we can stretch ourselves. In this chapter, we will discuss:

- the benefits of planning,
- how to create meaningful, effective plans, and
- the art of plan modification

I will not use these words a lot in this chapter, but you will see evidence of their application throughout.

Street Smarts

Goal: A broad primary outcome.
Strategy: The approach you take to achieve a goal.

Objective: A measurable step you take to achieve a strategy.

Tactic: A tool you use in pursuing an objective aligned with your strategy.

Why Plan

We plan because going with the flow ain't the wave. Anyone who has had success with that probably made room for going with the flow within their plan. When you have a very specific goal, you only benefit from getting specific about how you expect to spend your resources and chunks of your time even if you deviate from your original intentions. By doing so, you create a framework that can be adjusted over time to accommodate your reality.

Big Idea
Planning is important to reaching your desired results because it ensures steady growth and will help you prepare for your outcome.

By planning, I have been able to gracefully step into my new positions or fortunes without feeling shifty, odd, or like an impostor. If you have sprinted toward your goal with no plan in the past, here are seven reasons why you should consider creating a written plan moving forward.

1. **Better positioning.** No one plans to fail. Creating a plan will allow you

to create expectations for intermittent achievement. By doing this, you position yourself for success instead of just hoping and waiting for it.

2. **Progress mapping.** A great plan includes progress markers. These markers serve as a map from Point A to Point B and reveal the best pathway to meeting your goal.

3. **Clarity.** Setting a goal proves that we know what we want to achieve in a specific timeframe. Planning allows clarity in our short-term decision making which is integral in meeting that goal. Through planning, you become more efficient in your decision making as

you limit potential options that may have seemed endless before.

4. **Flexibility.** When planning, we allow ourselves the flexibility to adjust our actions in case of any unforeseen events. Flexibility helps us pivot when things go awry instead of giving up or taking the "L".

5. **Holistic improvement.** Through planning, you may be able to integrate some of your other goals. Sometimes planning for one goal can set you up for success in other areas in your life.

6. **Evaluation and control.** Planning allows you to have a methodology to refer back to in order to stay on

track, manage your progress, and evaluate your outcomes based on external factors.

7. **Calculated achievement.** Planning encourages you to do the necessary math and research before working toward any goal. By planning, you are able to figure out which tools (information, funds, counseling, ability, etc.) you'll need in order to complete certain actions in your plan.

The benefits of planning are endless. While creating your own plan, you may discover some benefits that are unique to your circumstance. Be sure to journal those in detail as a reminder of what planning has done for YOU.

Flip It on Its Head

Imagine you are planning a trip from Brooklyn, New York to Los Angeles, California. Naturally, you would start your trip by looking at where you are right now and figuring how to get from there to point B, C, and so on until you've reached your destination. This is how many of us plan our trips, and projects, but there is a more effective way to plan when it comes to meeting our long- and short-term goals.

"Sometimes you've gotta flip things on their head to get the right perspective." - Sarai W.

We are forward thinkers, therefore forward planners, but when it comes to completing goals, I have found it easier to plan backward. Backward planning is working from goal to start instead of start to goal. It allows us to:

1. accurately solidify our starting points,
2. clearly define motivating milestones,
3. and create our own sense of urgency.

Knowing what you want to complete 12 months from now (your goal) will help you work backward to figure out what you'll need to do six months, six weeks, and maybe even six days from now to complete that goal.

Write It Out
What do you need to have completed six months from now to be halfway toward your goal?

For the purposes of my example goal, ideally, I would have $500,000 in half a year (even though money typically doesn't work this way).

Write It Out

Now go even further. Create a milestone for each quarter (every 3 months) leading up to your goal. Create SMART goals to help you achieve each milestone in every quarter. Start at the end. What are the activities you need to do to get from quarter three to quarter four? From two to three? From one to two.

By this logic, my milestones are to have $1,000,000 by the end of Q4, $750,000 by the end of Q3, $500,000 by the end of Q2, and $250,000 by the end of Q1. Each milestone will get their own SMART goals.

With your SMART goals for each quarterly milestone listed, you should now be able to create monthly actions and establish timelines for the completion of each of those actions. It is here where you will realize whether or not your main goal can realistically be achieved in the time you've allotted.

Plan Modification: An Artform

But what if I get lost? What if things don't go exactly as planned? They never do.

Big Idea
Planning backward allows you to take control and adjust your actions at any point while still keeping you tethered when you unintentionally stray.

Sometimes you have to re-estimate your commitment. Maybe you forgot to factor in that you have children that need things. Maybe you have a demanding job. In planning for past goals, I've done everything from changing my diet to moving across the country to starting entire businesses. These are all life-changing actions that have their own benefits and consequences, so it is easy to get wrapped up in the actions themselves. BUT IS IT WORTH IT. You have the right to question the plan. It is yours. I constantly ask myself if my actions will help me reach my milestones if my milestones are the appropriate markers for success, and if the disruption it will cause to my life is worth it.

Manipulate your plan. Move dates around. Get creative about seeking resources. I personally like to make a game of things because that's in my nature. Ultimately, working your plan should not be a drag. This *is* your life we are talking about. Even though I don't expect things to come easy, I personally don't believe in suffering for success, but if you are the type that does, constantly question the worth of your suffering and if you find that it isn't worth it, consider modifying the plan.

Modifying my plan has never changed the goal. Your plan is its own little multiverse with various potential paths that lead to one outcome. Explore your options freely and without contempt. Each path you choose has something to teach you; even if the lesson is only, "that ain't your path, boo." Any "hustle" that you have seen out of me has been a symptom of me modifying my plan for one goal or another. This is why earlier in this text I urged you not to press your face against anyone's glass to get a closer look at how to get where they are. You don't know what they got going on up in there. You just know what you see; and covetous eyes are liars.

Talk is expensive.

The time I spent knowing what my goals and dilly-dallying around with them cost me in ways I don't care to share. You can write the vision until you are blue in the face. Set goals all day. Proud of you. But until you take action on the goal you prioritized in the previous chapter, those pieces of paper ain't gonna do squat for you, love. So, I hope you didn't think we were done.

I know taking action on your goals can get a little scary, but most worthwhile things are. **I AM AFRAID TO PUBLISH THIS BOOK!** But it is in your hands right now. Now that you have a plan, you have a framework for your OWN success. You did that!

Basically…

- Use your plan to create guidelines and smaller goals that aid in your ultimate desired results.
- Use your plan to ensure steady growth and prepare for your desired outcome.
- Plan backward to take control and adjust your actions at any point.
- Manipulate your plan as needed.

In the next chapter, we will explore some ways you may self-sabotage while working your plan.

START GHETTO

#startghetto

CHAPTER 5

AHT, AHT!

Chapter 5

Aht, Aht!

Oh no, baby. What is you doin'?

Now that you have solidified your goals and thought up your master plan, don't fuck it up on purpose. Sometimes we arm ourselves with all of the tools only to be taken out by our own cycle of self-sabotage.

I have become intimately acquainted with my own cycle of self-sabotage. There are three main factors that have stopped me from working my plan to the end. Goals that I have named, set, enthusiastically committed to, and planned for would fall flat because I let them (sometimes provoked them).

Outside of chronic depression and anxiety, sometimes I just be trippin'. For a long time, I was genuinely fearful of my own success, so I intentionally messed up good things. Other times I was contributing to my own destruction and didn't catch it until it was too late. In both cases, self-sabotage has created more work and added unnecessary pressure. My cycle of self-sabotage consisted of:

1. succumbing to my own **Limiting Beliefs,**

2. the Bad **Habits** I formed as a result, and
3. trying to escape the **Negative Environments** I found myself in thereafter creating more limiting beliefs and reinforcing pre-existing ones.

This cycle severely stunted my ability to get out of my head and get started on or finish things. Self-created obstacles exacerbated every circumstance that I found myself in when I let it. Here is how I work my way through thoughts and actions that sabotage my plan. I:

1. **Accepted** that I have go-to **limiting beliefs** that block my ambitions
2. **Acknowledge** the **bad habits** and destructive behaviors that

exacerbate and perpetuate my pre-existing circumstance and

3. Committed to meaningful introspective work and made intentional changes that enable me to **thrive in any environment.**

This combination of acceptance, acknowledgment, and commitment will help you address the situation-hopping discussed in Chapter 1 and put your self-sabotaging ways in check. You will be able to blossom, grow, and feel nourished wherever you are planted if you are willing to work through the feelings discussed in this chapter. Here, I will briefly discuss some no-nos (some aht-ahts if you will) that usually start us down our paths of destruction.

If any of the following methods of self-sabotage apply to you, work through them with a trusted advisor, or bring them up at your next therapy session. This list of tidbits is in no way intended to diagnose you or make you overthink, but to help you be more aware of thought patterns that may be unraveling your plan and undermining your goals.

On Scarcity Mindset

Just because we have to talk about it.

One thing that can contribute to your inability to sit in your ghetto and start from there is holding on to your scarcity mindset. Scarcity is the state of being in short supply. Some of our resources are *actually* scarce causing us to have an overwhelming feeling that there is never enough. This feeling can apply to one, a few, or multiple areas of our lives. Scarcity directs our minds to focus on — and be most attracted to — what we believe we are lacking. For example, someone who often feels starved of affection may automatically seek affection ravenously and to the point of ignoring other needs, true desires, and potential red flags.

A person who has a scarcity mindset may hold one or more of the following beliefs:

- There is never enough.
- The world is unfair.
- I need to be a "savage" to win.
- I benefit when others fail.
- I lose when others win.

Reflect + Check

Do I consciously or subconsciously hold any of these beliefs? Which belief(s), if any, stand out; and to which areas of my life do they apply?

These deep-seated feelings of lack can contribute to the following behaviors:

- Gossiping and judgment
- Comparing yourself
- Blaming others for your misfortune
- Selfishness with resources
- Big talk without follow-through

Reflect + Check
Do I exhibit any of these behaviors? What are the exact situations that cause me to behave this way? What do I attract or block as a result of this behavior?

Mindset can wildly affect the trajectory of your life. Frequent mindset checks will help you uncover the way you think about yourself and the world around you. You should frequently scan your mental and physical environments to see how your beliefs and behaviors help or hinder the way you learn, handle stress, create opportunities, recover from setbacks, and your general health.

The goal of this section is to help you transition from a state of scarcity to one of abundance. As I did with scarcity, I will share with you the beliefs and behaviors you may start to hold and exhibit when you actively embrace an abundance mindset. An abundance mindset is not to be confused with toxic positivity (although it is usually presented that way. This is simply about welcoming growth and exploring possibilities while still being able to live in reality.

A person who thinks abundantly may hold one or more of the following beliefs:

- There is more than enough for everyone.
- I should celebrate the success of others.
- My joy stems from gratitude.
- I win when others win and vice versa.
- There is more than one way to reach a goal.

Reflect + Check
Do I consciously or subconsciously hold any of these beliefs? Which belief(s), if any, stand out; and to which areas of my life do they apply?

Abundance beliefs contribute to the following behaviors:

- Being supportive of other's dreams
- Being grateful
- Sharing information and resources (with necessary boundaries) freely
- Abstaining from gossip and judgment
- Drawing inspiration — not comparison — from the accomplishments of others
- Being kind to oneself when accepting responsibility for failures

When scarcity is good. One of our biggest excuses for not setting or following through with goals is that there is never enough time. This is absolutely true. Time is a limited resource and most of us try not to waste it. When you learn to use this as fuel instead of allowing it to force you into inaction, it becomes easier to realize your goals. Time as a limited resource is a major caveat to an abundance mindset. I believe that it is perfectly okay to be frugal with time. When we are presented with too many options and pathways, scarcity prioritizes our choices so that we are not jumping at opportunities solely because they are presented to us.

One of my extremely motivated and successful entrepreneurial friends makes a daily schedule to guarantee the pursuit of her weekly and monthly goals. She noticed that when time is scarce, she becomes more focused on completing the tasks at hand because she knows she will not get to work on those goals again until the next time she's scheduled to do so. Since learning this, I have adopted this practice and recommend it to anyone who struggles with working just to feel busy.

Once you set goals, you have every right to be particular about how you allocate your time and what you give more or less time to. Honoring scarcity of time helps us confidently say "no" to things that do not propel us toward (or actively derails us from) our most pressing objectives. When I assign value to my time instead of insisting that I do not have enough, distractions that used to be pressing seem less tempting.

On Perfectionism

Perfectionism is commonly exalted as a positive trait rather than a flaw. However, an obsession with perfection has stopped even the most talented of us dead in our tracks. That is because, as a perfectionist, you need to be or appear perfect; and you are often paralyzed by your inability to do so. Even believing that there is such a thing as perfect leaves us flailing around on our backs like an overturned turtle.

Many perfectionists and the people around them believe that they are just striving to be the best versions of themselves. However, perfectionism can often be a protective mechanism and can be caused by and contribute to many of the other blockages presented in this text.

Some people may try to write off their perfectionism by calling themselves a "healthy perfectionist" and hiding behind their eye for detail. Healthy growth, though, cannot exist where the desire for perfection lives.

You may be a perfectionist or have tendencies if you believe that:

- You should avoid performing a task unless you know you can complete them perfectly
- A perfect end product is most important
- You should not accept credit for your own work if the end product is not perfect
- You should not begin a project until it can be done perfectly (see also: Procrastination)
- Taking more time than necessary to complete tasks.

Reflect + Check
Do I consciously or subconsciously hold any of these beliefs? Which belief(s), if any, stand out; and to which areas of my life do they apply?

Our perfectionist beliefs can contribute to the following behaviors:

- Spending too much time creating and revising projects that require little thought
- Getting angry or sad about being great, but not the best
- Finding difficulty being happy for others who are successful even when you are successful
- Comparing yourself unfavorably and unrealistically to others
- Avoiding a task because it is pointless to make an effort unless perfection can be achieved
- Focusing on the end product rather than the process of learning
- Avoiding healthy competition in fear that you will be outdone or exposed as imperfect.

Reflect + Check
Do I exhibit any of these behaviors? What are the exact situations that cause me to behave this way? What do I attract or block as a result of this behavior? What current obstacles exist because of my relationship with perfectionism?

On Lanes

Stay in yours. Not in the traditional sense where you are being told to keep your mouth shut and not have an opinion on certain things; but definitely in the way where you should mind your business. Sometimes we end up wanting what people have or have their goals and plans projected onto us because we weren't keeping our eyes on the road ahead of us. If you know where you are headed, it is wise to stay in your lane until switching lanes is a benefit and not a subtraction.

Posturing. Comparing yourself to and trying to keep up with people who have way more privilege than you is always going to be a losing game. What's more, people can always tell that you're doing it. A lot of my own battles with imposter syndrome came from faking it until I made it. Faking it, though, causes real debt, real depression, and real disorientation; all of which took me months out of my original plan and made me question my self-worth.

> **Reflect + Check**
> Am I trying to be someone I am not to appear more successful than I am?

Copying. Sometimes our inability to stay in our lane breeds a new problem —

copying. When we are in someone else's lane without a complete idea of where they are going and how they plan to get there, we end up having to wait for them to make their moves before we make ours. I can only address lane switching and copycats because I've been one. It was never malicious, but it happened and it created a ball of confusion. I used to think that if I wanted the success a person had, I should do what that person did. Duh. Go to the college they went to, work the jobs they've worked, etc. I was ill-advised. But I am glad to have experienced that so that I could confidently tell you to cut that shit out. If that message wasn't for you, pass it along to a friend.

Reflect + Check

Am I tempted by other people's journeys to their success to abandon my own?

On Willful Ignorance

Lesson dodging. If there is a lesson out there for you to learn, you are going to learn it. It will keep showing up in your life until you learn it. Do not attempt to avoid hard parts of your journey toward your goal to avoid hard lessons. Those same learned lessons will help you navigate future situations.

Reflect + Check
Do I attempt to avoid lessons? If so, how has this avoidance created undesirable repetition in my life?

Tunnel vision. Sometimes we want success so bad that we are willing to stay uninformed if we believe that the information will go against our mission. This kind of tunnel vision is often applauded, but there is a line that must be drawn. Try not to let your steadfastness turn into pigheadedness. Being presented with new information will often be valuable to your decision making.

Reflect + Check
Do I allow tunnel vision to deprive me of receiving new information?

On Burnout

Workaholichism. It ain't it. Take a break. Nothing about succeeding at a goal will be worth it if you are too tired or not healthy enough to enjoy it. There is no shame in tactfully dropping burdensome tasks that no longer serve you; and there is usually no reward for holding on to them if they do not align with your personal goals.

Reflect + Check
Do I take the breaks I need? Are there things that I can subtract from my workload to create less stress?

The struggle. You do not have to struggle in order for your success to be valid. For some of us, a difficult journey is a sign that we've paid our dues, therefore making us more deserving of our accomplishments. While any worthy goal will stretch you, you do not have to be broken to feel that you have earned your success. It is okay to accept ease where you can.

Reflect + Check
Do I glorify hard-earned success?

On Hoarding Information

If you have set a goal and devised a plan, you have all you need to take the first steps. It is normal to want to wait until we have enough information to dive headfirst into our plan. Research is an important part of formulating a plan. Research, though, can only take you so far. By using the information you have collected, you will begin to expose yourself to more of what you *didn't know* that you *didn't know* to make your research more targeted and useful.

Reflect + Check
Do I collect information without taking action on my findings?

On Ignoring Hardships

We all have uniquely valid hardships that must be acknowledged without being harped on. If a particular hardship is cited whenever something goes wrong in your plan, it may be more important to make dealing with that hardship a part of your plan so that it does not become an excuse. Some common hardships stem from these factors:

1. I don't have the money (lack of financial resources)

2. I'm unsure (lack of confidence in your plan or in yourself)

3. There are too many distractions (environmental and self-inflicted)

4. I don't know how (lack of education or skills)

5. I don't have help or encouragement (lack of support)

Understand that some of these things may always be true for you. Still, don't hyperbolize unfortunate situations and allow them to become excuses for your inaction. This is not to say that you are exaggerating your hardships, but you may be inserting them where they do not belong. I encourage you to make an effort to resolve any ill-feelings you have toward your lack of resources, confidence, distractions, education, and support. Therapy is a great place to start.

Reflect + Check
Do I amplify my hardships to fuel my excuse-making?

On Managing the Future

Anxiety boos, I'm talking to you. It is easy to confuse planning with managing the future. The fact is, you can only manage yourself; and even that is a big task. Planning does not mean every little thing will go your way. The more you welcome the unknown, the fewer scars you will have for trying to resist it.

Reflect + Check

Do I attempt to manage the future? Does this cause any difficulties when attempting to carry out my plan?

On Permission

Sometimes you need permission for things. Sometimes you don't. It is just that simple. I have found that people who have problems with permission believe that they never need it or that they always need it. If you find that you always need it, work on building your confidence and strengthening your voice. If you never need it, work on respecting boundaries and having reverence for new territory.

Reflect + Check
What is my relationship with permission? If I lean one way or the

other, how can I create balance in this area?

On Starting Scared

I recommend that you never fucking do this. People who give this advice may look back on a pivotal moment of their life and say that they "started scared", but it is so easy to leave out either:

- the damage that was done as a result of starting scared or
- their own personal motivations to start despite their crippling fear.

Sometimes we sabotage ourselves by doing things before we are ready. If you are truly afraid, explore your fears. Decide for yourself or with an advisor which fears are valid and work toward becoming less afraid. You have the right to create a plan that doesn't trigger debilitating fear.

Reflect + Check
Have I truly started anything scared? What was the outcome of that situation?

On Absorbing Feedback

Do not. Criticism and praise are tricky to navigate, especially when you started off unsure and insecure. It is important not to absorb either or let them influence how you feel about yourself. You are never as good as the overly gratuitous praise you receive, and you are never as bad as the negative criticism.

Reflect + Check

Have I allowed feedback to go to my head?

Many of these roadblocks show up in the conversations I have with my clients at all levels of success. Someone can be right at the edge of glory and report feelings of not being good enough or being too wiped out to go on. Often, not even comforting words and facts can pull them out of their spiral. That is how powerful our self-sabotage can be. These blockages can eventually lead to habits that allow our cycle of self-sabotage to seem never-ending, ultimately taking away our own abilities to pursue our goals. Again, talk to someone. Sometimes it is healthy for a third party to help coax you out of your head.

Basically…

- Accept your limiting beliefs.
- Acknowledge the bad habits you form as a result of your beliefs.
- Seek help when necessary and possible.

In the next chapter, we will discuss self-awareness, self-acceptance, and self-mastery.

START GHETTO

#startghetto

CHAPTER 6

LEAN IN

Chapter 6
Lean In

Your True Nature vs. Your Goals

What does my true nature have to do with my goals?
Why does my true nature matter when I am trying to get from point A to point B?

Everything. Throughout this book, I have referenced "your true nature" without really explaining what that is, how to find it, or how being aware of mine has changed my life. That is because *it is what it is and what is* understood doesn't need to be explained. However, for the purposes of not being intentionally cryptic, I will describe the thick book that is my true nature as **Healthy, Glorious Fucklessness.** This title pretty much sums up how I have leaned into some of my most glorified and criticized attributes and turned them into my superpower.

Even before I was fully aware of this, I have experienced the best possible outcome when I made decisions that were in line with my true nature. When I go against my nature, it definitely catches up with and weighs down my mind, body, and spirit.

I make decisions that are going to grant me harmony; even if it looks stupid to onlookers at the time that the decision is made. This is the ultimate respect I can pay to myself and the longest lifeline I can give my goals. Moving in total alignment and obedience with my true nature has opened doors for me that I didn't even know I wanted to walk through. It has strengthened my ability to say no to things that don't serve me and yes to more things that do. This same alignment, though, has cost me more relationships and 'opportunities' than I care to count. In the end, everything has worked out for the best because there is no price you can put on walking in your truth and obeying yourself.

Sometimes the happiness we wish to create for ourselves (and the way we go about seeking that happiness) is not in alignment with our true nature. Whatever your roles, goals, and plans are, keep your true nature in mind. It is okay if you cannot put words to what that is, but deep down, we all know. Whether or not you choose to acknowledge your true nature — yourself stripped bare — is the question.

Happiness and contentment are your baseline — your nature. Your nature is different from mine and the next person's, but what is the same across the board is that our ecosystems are often disrupted by the unhappiness that we create and that we let in while pursuing what is already within us. You do not have to chase or search for the natural themes of your life. It will constantly unfold as long as you are diligent about inquiring within. Until you are willing to become unraveled, you will never experience actual contentment.

I cannot teach you to be content. I can only encourage you to lean in when you discover contentment. As you have probably figured out, this chapter is more contemplative than instructional. Discovering the nature of self is not a destination or a goal. In fact, it is the anti-goal. Your true nature is who you are when you are not creating layers of suffering with your convictions and projections about what life should be. It is who you are when you submit to experiencing life rather than getting stuck in your thoughts about life.

In this chapter, you will begin to understand how simple self-inquiries can lead to self-awareness, self-acceptance, and eventually self-mastery. **Healthy, Glorious Fucklessness** is what I found through self-mastery. It is my way of acknowledging happiness and contentment as my default. Once I stopped chasing happiness, I was able to set more sincere and authentic goals that were easier to pursue and complete with enthusiasm.

Self-Awareness

Internal self-awareness. How do you understand yourself? How clearly do you see your own values, aspirations, your place in your environment? How do you view your thoughts, feelings, behaviors, strengths, and weaknesses, and impact on others? This is your internal self-awareness or your inner world. Our inner world is the part of our self-awareness that is associated with career and relationship satisfaction, how we control ourselves in personal and social situations, and happiness. It also impacts our mental health.

External self-awareness. Do you understand how others view you? I've noticed that people who know how they are perceived by others are usually prompted to look inward more often than people who are oblivious to the same.

Becoming externally aware can be just the mirror you need in order to trigger a much-needed deep dive.

I recommend playing an active role in your self-awareness. There are few things worse than the existential crisis caused by someone pulling your card. Make an effort to validate your own existence before someone makes you question everything about it.

On Detachment

I detach. A lot. Not spitefully or with malice, but simply because I can. It is how I am able to welcome small reminders of who I am and why I am here. Every once in a while, I have to put everything down. I allow my roles, responsibilities, interest, goals, status, and happiness to briefly fade away as I become zero. Uncountable.

Nothing. This can take a few minutes or a few days, but it is here where I am able to become one with who I truly am.

Sometimes we hold on to things because we are attached to them. Not because we like them or because they are serving us, but because our attachment has bound them to our being. Maybe you hate your career, but still, you find yourself taking pride in putting your job title in your email signature. Maybe your spouse is trash, but you find yourself posing for pictures with your left ring finger front and center.

We wrap ourselves in all of these ideas about who we (and other people) think we are, and we forget that we are none of them. The truth is that most attachment is about control. We enjoy being able to shape our own narratives even if that means deceiving ourselves along the way. The control we think we have, though, is an illusion. Your true nature will always find you and show up at the most inconvenient occasions.

Many of us may find it difficult to detach because we enjoy stability and comfort. We like knowing what to expect from our surroundings. Maybe this has caused you to operate on autopilot? Frequent detachment has allowed me to gradually merge into who I am and helps me navigate new surroundings.

Listen to Your Loudest Self

Have you ever felt like you were screaming, and no one could hear you? This is usually caused by us not listening to *ourselves.* That 'no one' that isn't listening to your screams may be you. Or maybe you are screaming over your truth; ignoring your true needs, values, and motivators. Our needs, values, and motivators have power over our decisions and actions.

Affirm Your Damn Self

Other people's affirmations have never resonated with me. This text will not supply you with affirmations because your affirmative self-talk should be unique to you. We all have both negative and positive core beliefs that we've picked up in our formative years. Acknowledge them both. Below is a list of general positive beliefs that I hold that have helped me create and curate positive thoughts and behaviors that are self-supporting. Here is the technique I use to identify my own core beliefs. Knowing my core beliefs has helped me create my very own affirmations.

You can find your core beliefs by working backward. This involves you paying attention and following each thought back to where it came from. For this initial exercise, you will be required to collect some positive and negative thoughts you have about yourself. For example:

Positive: I'm always helping people out.
Negative: I can never finish anything on time.

Ask yourself, "What does that mean about me?" Your answer should describe you as a person. For example:

Positive: I am helpful.
Negative: I am lazy.

Keep asking, "What does that mean about me?" until you get to the core belief.

Positive: I am an asset.
Negative: I am weak-minded.

I made these answers up. Your answers should look a lot different.

Our core beliefs dictate the rules we live by. So, if you believe that you are an asset, you will create rules that reflect your usefulness. If you believe you are weak-minded, your rules will reflect that as well. Your genuine positive and negative affirmations will form as a result of your own internal government. You can use these affirmations — the things you already believe — as a springboard to create new affirmations self-supporting.

Self-Supporting Behaviors

Affirmations have to be put into action. You have to DO something to make words work. I am the last person to speak against vibrations and law of attraction, but that is only half of the tea. While you are trusting the universe to smack you into alignment consider taking small steps to help the cosmos along. Some self-supporting behaviors that fortify my affirmations include:

- Consuming Goodness - Take in food, media, people, etc. that match what you said you want for yourself
- Checking Yourself - Put yourself back in your place when you are behaving in a way that doesn't align with who you are.
- Welcoming Mistakes - Allow yourself to mess up, recover, and try again.
- Practicing Gratitude - Say thank you for the things that are in your life. By doing

this, you reveal to yourself what you value and what is going unnoticed in your life.

- Being Transparent - The more you hide, the more you have to hide. Be transparent with yourself and others. You will learn to trust yourself and others will trust you, too.
- Duplicating Success - Learn to keep doing the things that work. Turn your wins into systems.
- Acknowledging Your Capabilities - Use your talents and skills when they are needed.
- Acknowledging Your Shortcomings - Accept when you are bad at things. This is the first step to becoming good (if that is the mission).
- Addressing Your Trauma - Go to therapy.
- Asking for Help - Get help even before you need help. Help is not a last resort.

Actively working on my own self-awareness has helped me with self-acceptance, self-mastery, and (eventually) **Healthy, Glorious, Fucklessness.** By truly leaning into who I am and knowing when to practice self-obedience, I have been able to achieve what ghetto little me thought was out of reach.

Just A Little More Tea

I used to take offense to being called "inspirational." When people would call me "the *I* word" I'd hear, "if even *you* could do xyz, then so could I." It sounds ridiculous to me now, but a slightly less secure me felt bothered by the notion that what I had accomplished couldn't be that hard for the simple fact that *I* was able to do it.

These feelings came rushing back while writing this book. The hardest part about pouring over each of these pages has been that most days I don't feel qualified to advise anyone. Outside of setting, pursuing, and eventually crushing goals, my life has been a ghetto jamboree. This is why for so long, I've been in vehement opposition to being anyone's inspiration. The people are right, though. I shouldn't have been gainfully employed for years after dropping out of Howard University where I BULLSHAT my way toward a degree I never finished. Nor should I have been able to build several online platforms (that people actually find useful).

While I may not consider myself the best role model, I eventually had to unburden myself of my imagined *impostorship* and accept that I *am* an inspiration. If I am being completely honest with myself and anyone who has stumbled upon this text, the world isn't exactly an oyster to unmarried, 30-year-old, Black women with no college degree. So, now when someone calls me 'inspirational,' I graciously accept the compliment because whether they mean it sincerely or backhandedly, they ain't lying.

Before I earned accolades of my own (and even some time thereafter) I, too, was inspired by little ghetto girls that went on to do *big things.* I watched in wonderment as they publicly secured their bags; always mystified by their ability to do *that* when their lives were like *this.* So, it is no real shock that people might be thinking the same thing about me.

I decided to write *Start Ghetto* because that's the only advice I have for you at this time. It is how I answer anyone who wants to know where and how to start doing "the thing." I wanted to get this philosophy down on paper as proof to my future self that I believed this *waaaay* back when; and that it isn't something cute for my future self to say when she is too paid and can't be bothered.

Even before I had the words for it, starting ghetto has been the way I moved through this world. It is how I've been able to make myself at home in spaces many people who share one or more of my circumstances will never even consider obtainable. Now that I've accepted starting ghetto as a superpower (and not a dirty little secret of which to be ashamed), I can confidently share it with you and anyone else who is seeking guidance in the messy, clumsy, sometimes terrifying art of getting started.

This book is about growth — mainly mine. As much as I am a teacher here, I am the student. Through writing *Start Ghetto*, I realized that I couldn't teach you anything until I became comfortable with my uncertainty. I could not comfortably share what I do know if I didn't accept that there is so much more to learn.

I set out to No book is going to help you get your shit together; especially not this one. At the time of this book's publishing, I am in one of my thickest ghettos.

I wish I could tell you that I was in the best possible space when I wrote these words. Is that how you pictured it? Me perched atop my high horse with my shit together (being an inspiration)? While that would be cute, it is far from the truth. I wrote the bulk of this book while having issues in my primary relationship, grieving the loss of a sibling, quarantined in my mother's basement, and fighting overt racism — 100% opposite from how and where I thought I would pen the entire framework for my coaching practice. Sometimes being thrown into undesirable situations is exactly what we need to take action towards what we want. There is nothing to lose at rock bottom. I needed to be here. I needed to throw away the first version of this book. I needed to confront myself in isolation and reconnect with my true nature. The same basement that felt like a cell to me a few years ago, has been my sanctuary. It feels good to know that even in sanctuary, there is nowhere else to go but up.

Thank You for Kicking It With Me

If you enjoyed this book, please consider leaving a review on **Amazon and**

wherever else this book is sold and/or reviewable. Your review will help other people find this book and future books in this series.

If you would like to engage with other readers, use the hashtag #**startghetto** (wherever hashtags are relevant these days) so we can all enjoy your book photos, commentary, and quotes.

If you are not on socials, you can send your commentary, reviews, and inquiries to **startghetto@latetrao.com.**

Please share this book with anyone who has trouble starting and finishing things (especially if they need goal setting help).

This book was meant to be a straightforward guide to getting it done, but it does not address every reader specifically. If you would like help identifying, setting, and pursuing personal, professional, and/ or creative goals, let's do it together!

Visit **startghetto.latetrao.com** to keep up with the *Start Ghetto* book series.

START GHETTO

#startghetto

CHAPTER 7

WHAT'S NEXT?

Chapter 7

What's Next

Creating Your Start Ghetto Action Group

Creating an action group with a few trusted, like-minded individuals can help you add life to the Big Ideas in this book. Together, you can dive deeper into the ideas covered in this text and provide each other with real-life examples of obstacles and growth. Each person in your action group

This chapter outlines recommended prompts that will help you lead and structure each session. You may add to or subtract from the suggested prompts in order to best suit your group. Ultimately, your discussions and activities should reflect the needs of your action group.

An action group of two or more can serve as a simple book club where you strictly discuss the text or an intimate accountability group. However, feel free to cover the material alone and turn the discussion starters into journal prompts.

Meeting 1. What's the Thing?

Introduction: Introduce yourselves and the reason you've picked up *Start Ghetto*. Ask each member they hope to gain from participating in this action group?

Reading: Chapter 1. "Let's Pre-gin"

Discussion:

- What do you want to start or complete?
- Why haven't you started the thing you've identified?
- What do you think contributes to your inaction or incomplete actions?

Before You Go: What part(s) of this chapter spoke directly to you? Continue your discussion based on group responses.

Homework: Reflect on possible reasons you've made to not start, pursue or finish something. In your opinion, which reasons are valid? Which were excuses?

Meeting 2. Where Are You?

Introduction: Share any relevant reflections from your homework.

Reading: Chapter 2. "You Are Here"

Discussion:

- Have you actually set goals for the things you've wanted?
- Which reason(s) for not setting goals do you most identify with?

Before You Go: How has failure to set goals or setting the wrong goals impacted your ability to accomplish things?

Homework: Reflect on times you've set "the wrong goals?" What were the outcomes?

Meeting 3. Down to Business.

Introduction: Discuss relevant observations from your homework.

Reading: Chapter 3. "Get Goalsy"

Discussion:

- What are your roles?
- Do they align with or conflict with your goals?

Before You Go: Which goal would you like to prioritize first?

Homework: Consider your goal? Can or should it be broken down into smaller goals?

Meeting 4. What's the Plan?

Introduction: If you realized that your goal could be smaller, share your goal breakdowns with each other. Ask each other any questions that may arise.

Reading: Chapter 4. "Get Planny"

Discussion:

- What does working backward look like for your goal?
- Does your plan reveal any flaws in your goal or the time you've given yourself to complete it?

Before You Go: What potential obstacles do you anticipate while working your plan?

Homework: Consider which actions you would need to take to reach each milestone in your plan?

Meeting 5. Keep an Eye Out For...

Introduction: Have each member share some of the actions they have to take to reach their specified milestones.

Reading: Chapter 5. "Aht, Aht!"

Discussion:

- Which bad habits are you working on or around?

Homework: Consider your plan in the context of the entire text, and your Action Group Meetings. Create a list of things you wish to be held accountable for by your Action Group.

Read Chapter 6 on your own.

Meeting 6. The Exchange

Ask group members to share their lists. Group members may choose to share some list items with some members, all list items with all members, or keep the lists to themselves. Members who agree to hold each other accountable should create and enter a formal or informal accountability contract.

START GHETTO

REFERENCE

#startghetto BIG IDEAS

REMEMBERING WHAT'S IMPORTANT

Reference

Big Ideas

Here are some of the main thoughts presented in this text. If others jump out at you, highlight them and add them here.

Chapter 1.

1. You deserve and can absolutely aspire to, work for, and earn success

even if you don't beat your odds or escape your ghetto.

2. It is important that we refrain from being chased out of our circumstances and learn to thrive in them.

3. New circumstances do not guarantee a new you.

4. *Start Ghetto* is a charge. It requires you to manually pinpoint where you are and take inventory of what you have instead of ignoring the unpretty parts about your life in the name of automatic growth and forward movement.

5. Finding better circumstances is not the goal. The thing you want is the goal.

6. This text exists to help you move enthusiastically towards your wildest dreams; shamelessly and unapologetically as yourself; even when there are people who think you should not or cannot (and even if that person is you).

Chapter 2.

7. Don't perpetuate your own skepticism about the goals you want to set.

8. Your fear of failure could be causing you to fail.

9. Your comfort zone is the perfect place to set new goals.

10. Don't let your need for instant gratification seep into the vision you have for your life.

11. Hanging onto previous disappointments can stop you from setting goals.

Chapter 3.

12. Make your goal a brief, clear statement of an outcome to be reached within a specific timeframe.

13. Always back your goal with an important why.

14. Prioritize your main goal by determining what is most urgent or what can help you take steps towards completing other goals.

15. Understand that your goals may not always align with your interests.

16. Check all of your goals against SMART for the best possible outcome.

Chapter 4.

17. Use your plan to create guidelines and smaller goals that aid in your ultimate desired results.

18. Use your plan to ensure steady growth and prepare for your desired outcome.

19. Plan backward to take control and adjust your actions at any point.

20. Manipulate your plan as needed.

Chapter 5.

21. Accept your limiting beliefs.

22. Acknowledge the bad habits you form as a result of your beliefs.

23. Seek help when necessary and possible.

START GHETTO

REFERENCE

#startghetto REFLECT + CHECK

EXERCISING YOUR INNER VOICE

Reference

Reflect + Check

You may use the following inquiries to check in on yourself or your coaching clients. Each question is best answered honestly or not at all. You may choose to keep these answers private until you are ready to discuss your answers.

Chapter 1.

1. What is it that I don't like about this place (my circumstance), and how you exist within it?

2. Call your desires by name. Say it out loud. Claim it for yourself. Don't hesitate.

Chapter 2.

3. Am I skeptical about my ability to achieve? If skepticism is my reason for not setting goals, what have I done to contribute to my own disbelief? How will I work towards finding more of the role models I need and less of the ones I want?

4. Am I allowing fear to talk me out of my desire to ______?

5. What role does fear play in my goal setting habits?

6. Think about some things in your life that came quick and easy. Maybe it was last night's dinner. Maybe it was a relationship (oop). Maybe it was a job you chose over another because it came easier than the one you really wanted. How are those things working out for you? Was it the best meal you ever had? Do you still rock with what's her/his name? Do you still want that other job?

Chapter 5.

7. Do I consciously or subconsciously hold any scarcity or perfectionist beliefs? Which belief(s), if any, stand

out; and to which areas of my life do they apply?

8. Do I exhibit any scarcity or perfectionist behaviors? What are the exact situations that cause me to behave this way? What do I attract or block as a result of this behavior? What current obstacles exist because of my relationship with perfectionism?

9. Am I trying to be someone I am not to appear more successful than I am?

10. Am I tempted by other people's journeys to their success to abandon my own?

11. Do I attempt to avoid lessons? If so, how has this avoidance created undesirable repetition in my life?

12. Do I allow tunnel vision to deprive me of receiving new information?

13. Do I take the breaks I need? Are there things that I can subtract from my workload to create less stress?

14. Do I glorify hard-earned success?

15. Do I collect information without taking action on my findings?

16. Do I attempt to manage the future? Does this cause any difficulties when attempting to carry out my plan?

17. What is my relationship with permission? If I lean one way or the other, how can I create balance in this area?

18. Have I truly started anything scared? What was the outcome of that situation?

19. Have I allowed feedback to go to my head?

START GHETTO

REFERENCE

#startghetto

WRITE IT OUT

GETTING IT DOWN
IN INK

Reference

Write it Out

Here are a few journal entry prompts. Feel free to Feel free to create your own!

Chapter 2.

1. Do I have access to people of similar backgrounds and/or

circumstances that have set or completed similar goals? If not, can I gain that access? If I do, do I intentionally surround myself with those people?

2. What current obstacles exist because of my fear of failure? How will failure continue to disrupt my life?

3. Write down a list of things you haven't done because of your feelings of inadequacy. These list items can be anything from finally drawing a picture on that canvas you bought to cutting a thirteen song album in the voice memos of your phone. Put it out there.

4. Make a list of all the things that you do that you could afford to cut back on for the purposes of pursuing your goals. These things are usually trivial and mostly enjoyable. Order your list from most enjoyable to least enjoyable and try to eliminate the things you dislike the most first.

Chapter 3.

5. Create a list of all the different roles you have in life.

6. Based on the six listed areas of influence, which of your personal interests come to mind? Your personal interests can be experiences you've had and would like more of or some things you're curious about. You may find that

some interests can be listed in more than one area of influence.

7. Set one specific goal in each area that you'd like to accomplish within the next 12 months (we'll keep the timeframe short for now but you can extend it if you need to). Your goal should be broad, general, tangible, descriptive, and measurable by quality and quantity. Perhaps your goals align with your interest. Maybe they don't. Maybe you will identify new interests while setting your goals.
   Consider each goal separately. For every goal you've listed, create a list of your motivations for completing each goal. You can answer the following questions if you need help getting started with your lists.

Why is this goal important
right now?
What *benefits* will I enjoy
once I achieve this goal?

8. What do you need to have completed six months from now to be halfway toward your goal?
9. Now go even further. Create a milestone for each quarter (every 3 months) leading up to your goal. Create SMART goals to help you achieve each milestone in every quarter. Start at the end. What are the activities you need to do to get from quarter three to quarter four? From two to three? From one to two.

REFERENCE

#startghetto STREET SMARTS

KEY TERMS

Reference
Street Smarts

These terms are defined for the purposes of this text.

Goal /gōl/
a broad primary outcome.

Ghet·to /ˈgedō/
the all-encompassing term for any physical, mental, or emotional space in which you

feel restricted, stuck, and unable to make purpose-driven progress.

Mean·time Meas·ures /ˈmēnˌtīm ˈmeZHərz/
the things we do while waiting to do the things we want to do.

Meh /me/
expressing a lack of interest or enthusiasm.

Mile·stone /ˈmīlˌstōn/
an action or event marking a significant change or stage in development.

Ob·jec·tive /əbˈjektiv/
a measurable step you take to achieve a strategy.

Role Mod·el /rōl ˈmädl/
a person looked to by others as an example to be imitated.

SMART
an acronym that stands for Specific, Measurable, Attainable/ Achievable, Relevant/Realistic, and Timely in reference to goals.

Strat·e·gy /ˈstradəjē/
the approach you take to achieve a goal.

Tac·tic /ˈtaktik/
a tool you use in pursuing an objective aligned with your strategy.

The Thing /T͟Hē,T͟Hə tHiNG/
a specific, strong, and personal desired outcome.

Un·for·tu·nate Nows /ˌən'fôrCH(ə)nət nouz/
moments of ambiguous hardship.

#startghetto

Whys /(**h**)**wīz**/
reasons or motives that back your goals.

La Tetra O. helps creatives and entrepreneurs get out of their heads and get started. Learn more at STARTGHETTO.LATETRAO.COM

Made in the USA
Middletown, DE
06 November 2023